REAL WORLD MATH: HEALTH AND WELLNESS

RESTAURANTS BY THE NUMBERS

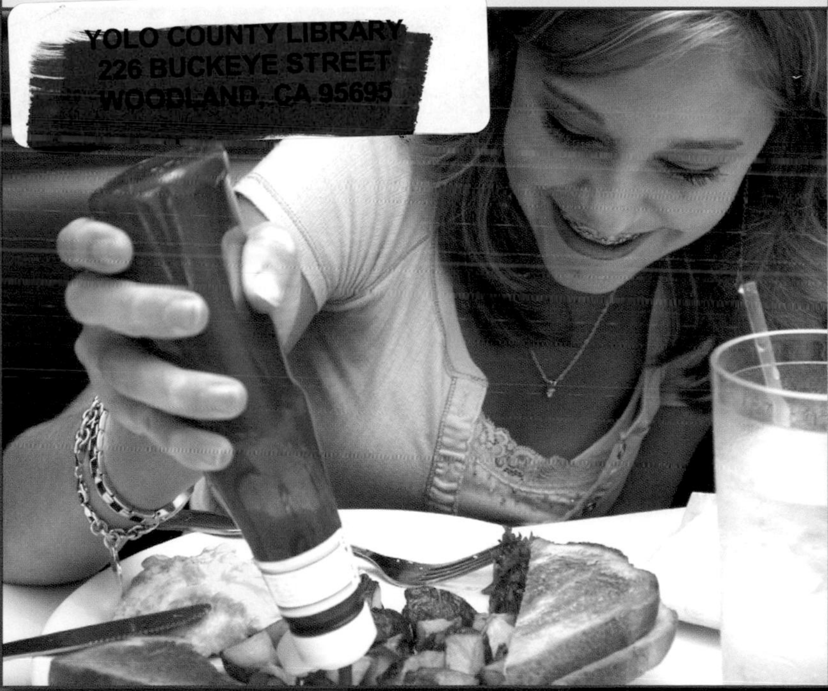

Cecilia Minden

Cherry Lake Publishing
Ann Arbor, Michigan

Published in the United States of America by Cherry Lake Publishing
Ann Arbor, MI
www.cherrylakepublishing.com

Math Adviser: Tonya Walker, MA, Boston University

Nutrition Adviser: Steven Abrams, MD, Professor of Pediatrics, Baylor College of Medicine, Houston, Texas

Photo Credits: Page 9, © Comstock Select/CORBIS; page 16, © Robert Wallis/CORBIS; page 20, Photo Courtesy of U. S. Department of Agriculture

Library of Congress Cataloging-in-Publication Data
Minden, Cecilia.
Restaurants by the numbers / by Cecilia Minden.
p. cm.
ISBN-13: 978-1-60279-009-4 (hardcover)
ISBN-10: 1-60279-009-4 (hardcover)
1. Arithmetic—Juvenile literature. 2. Restaurants—Juvenile literature. 3. Food—Miscellanea—Juvenile literature. I. Title.
QA115.M565 2007
513—dc22 2007004672

Cherry Lake Publishing would like to acknowledge the work of The Partnership for 21st Century Skills. Please visit www.21stcenturyskills.org *for more information.*

Table of Contents

CHAPTER ONE

Dining Out

Sometimes a quick slice of take-out pizza is dinner for busy family members.

It's Friday night and your sister has a basketball game. Mom will be late getting home and Dad just walked in the door from a business trip. There is no time to cook and you don't want to eat leftovers. It seems like the perfect evening to eat out!

Meals out can be anything from a slice of pizza to an elegant dinner. Does your family have a favorite place? No matter what kind of food you prefer, eating in a restaurant is convenient and gives you a chance to try new foods.

Many families go to restaurants to celebrate major events. Perhaps it's your grandmother's birthday, or maybe you aced a difficult history test. People also will eat out because it's a quick, easy alternative to preparing a meal on their own. Cooking at home can be fun and save money, but it sometimes involves a lot of work.

Eating out is fun, but remember that what you eat affects your health. Families often eat less fruits and vegetables in restaurants. They tend to **consume** more foods high in fats, sugars, and salt. These ingredients aren't bad for you in small amounts, but too much of them can be bad for your health.

The term *restaurant* comes from the French word *restaurer*, which means "to restore." The first restaurant opened in Paris, France, in 1765. The owner, A. Boulanger, served a variety of soups that helped restore customers to good health.

REAL WORLD MATH CHALLENGE

According to Dr. William Doherty at the University of Minnesota, "Twenty-three percent of meals are eaten in restaurants. Of those made at home, 26 percent used **convenience foods**, and 17 percent used supermarket or restaurant takeout."

What percentage of meals is not eaten in restaurants?

What percentage of meals made at home did not use convenience foods or takeout items?

(Turn to page 29 for the answers)

It is okay to eat a burger with bacon and cheese and fries once in a while, but you should try to stick to meals that contain less fat and more fruits and vegetables on most days.

REAL WORLD MATH CHALLENGE

Most people eat three meals each day.

Since there are seven days in a week, how many meals is that each week?

If people eat 23 percent of their meals in restaurants, about how many meals is that each week?

Since there are 52 weeks in a year, about how many meals is that each year?

(Turn to page 29 for the answers)

Portion size is another problem when eating out. Restaurants know that people like a bargain and will frequently try to attract customers with offers of bigger serving sizes at cheaper costs. Though this tactic might help you save money, it also can add up to a lot of extra **calories**.

Does all this mean you shouldn't get meals from restaurants? No way! More and more restaurants are serving healthier foods as Americans grow increasingly conscious of what they eat. There are many ways you can make **nutritious** choices and still enjoy a delicious breakfast, lunch, or dinner at a restaurant. Knowing how to read and evaluate a menu will get you off to the right start!

It is easy to eat too much food at an all-you-can eat buffet restaurant.

CHAPTER TWO

Menu Please!

Talk to your server and find out if you can substitute healthier items, for example, a side of fruit or steamed vegetables instead of French fries.

Are you a clever detective? Reading a menu can be like reading a mystery. You search for clues that will help you choose a healthy meal. Menus list all the different foods served at a restaurant. Appetizers, salads, and soups are usually

Foods that are deep-fried in oil are high in fat and calories and should be eaten only occasionally.

described at the beginning of the menu, as these are foods we normally eat at the beginning of a meal. Next comes information about various entrées. *Entrée* is a French word that means the "main dish" of a meal. Desserts are eaten at the end of a meal and are sometimes listed on a separate menu.

When you look over the menu and talk to restaurant staff, pay special attention to how food is prepared. Knowing the meaning behind a few simple cooking terms provides important clues. *Fried* food is submerged in hot oil. *Marinated* items are often soaked in oil before being cooked. The oil

Need extra clues about what foods to order to create the best nutritional balance? Visit www.MyPyramid.gov to learn more about how to choose healthy meals. The food pyramid there places foods in the following categories: grains, vegetables, fruits, milk, meat and beans, and oils.

Grains are foods made from wheat, rice, oats, barley, and other whole grains. Vegetables can be fresh, frozen, canned, or dried. Whole fruits or 100 percent fruit juice are a part of the fruit group. Milk and products made from milk are in the milk group. Foods in the meat and bean group include meat, **poultry**, fish, nuts, eggs, and beans. The oils category features liquid oils such as olive and canola oil, and solid fats such as butter.

The Web site also includes information on serving sizes and how many servings you need from each food group every day.

Creamy salad dressings and croutons add a lot of calories to a salad.

used to prepare these foods adds extra fat and calories to your meal. Gravies, sauces, and creamy salad dressings can have the same effect. None of these foods are bad for you if you eat them occasionally, but most restaurants have more nutritionally balanced selections that are better for you to choose on a regular basis.

Scan menus for *whole grain* breads or pastas. Select meat or fish that is *baked, broiled,* or *grilled. Fresh* or *steamed* vegetables are good choices when it comes to picking a side dish. *Low-fat* is the clue word when choosing salad dressings, frozen yogurt, ice cream, or milk. These cooking methods and alternative ingredients go a long way toward reducing your calorie count and solving the mystery of how to order a healthy restaurant meal.

Don't be shy with restaurant staff—this is *your* meal, and you need to take personal responsibility for making sure that it's as healthy and tasty as possible. Servers can often aid you in solving the great menu mystery. Ask how food is prepared, if it's not clearly stated on the menu. Check if you can substitute one item for another if the swap will make a difference in nutritional value. For example, try to replace an order of fries with a green salad. Ask for a plain baked potato topped with low-fat dressing or **salsa** (instead of butter and sour cream). Request that sauces be served on the side so you can control serving size. If there's food left over, ask for a doggie bag so that nothing goes to waste and you can enjoy more of your meal later.

Real World Math Challenge

Jay goes to an Italian restaurant for dinner and orders **fettuccine Alfredo**. This dish has 1,140 calories per serving. Jay normally takes in about 2,000 calories each day.

What percent of his total daily calories did he have in this single meal?

If Jay had chosen to split his entrée with his sister and had ordered a mixed greens salad (50 calories) with low-fat dressing (20 calories), what would have been the difference in his calorie intake?

(Turn to page 29 for the answers)

Fettucine Alfredo is pasta in a sauce made with butter, cream, and cheese.

CHAPTER THREE

Do the Math: Fast Food

Many young people enjoy eating at fast food restaurants.

Did you know that even ancient Romans enjoyed fast food? If you needed a quick meal to go, you could purchase bread and olives from a stand in the marketplace. Thousands of years later, fast-food restaurants

Fast food isn't found just in the United States. China is now home to 100 Pizza Huts. On opening day in Kuwait City, Kuwait, the line for the McDonald's drive-through was more than 7 miles (11 kilometers) long.

A family enjoys a meal at the first McDonald's restaurant in India. The restaurant opened in 1996.

have taken the world by storm. In the United States, kids ages 6 to 14 eat in fast-food restaurants 157 million times a month!

So are you ready to hit the local drive-through? Surf the Internet before you surf the menu. Most fast-food restaurants list the nutritional values of the foods they serve on their Web page. Some restaurants even have this information at the counter where you order. Review these details, and make an effort to avoid foods that are high in calories, fat, salt, and sugar. If you can, try to select items that are baked or grilled or feature low-fat ingredients, and that represent all the food groups.

Real World Math Challenge

Lin orders a kid's meal at a fast-food restaurant. As a side, she can choose between fries or apple slices with low-fat caramel dip. The fries are 250 calories, and the apples with caramel dip have 100 calories.

What is the difference in calories between these two side dishes?

Lin usually consumes about 2,000 calories a day. What percentage of her daily calorie intake is represented in each of the side dishes?

(Turn to page 29 for the answers)

REAL WORLD MATH CHALLENGE

One day, Marcus decides to eat all of his meals at a fast-food restaurant. He chooses the following items:

Breakfast: Sausage and egg biscuit (500 calories), hash browns (140 calories), and a medium orange juice (180 calories)

Lunch: Large hamburger (420 calories), medium fries (380 calories), and a medium cola (210 calories)

Dinner: Chicken strips (380 calories), small fries (250 calories), a medium orange drink (240 calories), and a hot fudge sundae (330 calories)

What is the total number of calories that Marcus consumes by making these meal selections?

If his normal calorie intake is 2,300 calories, how many more calories does Marcus consume on this particular day?

(Turn to page 29 for the answers)

Of course, no one can resist a creamy chocolate shake every now and again, so just keep in mind that bigger isn't always better. If your favorite treat is high in calories or foods that you only need a little of each day, simply order a smaller size.

CHAPTER FOUR

Do the Math: Trying New Foods

You can enjoy a gyros plate at a Greek restaurant.

Everyone has a favorite burger joint or pizza parlor, but it's always a good idea to get out and try new foods. **Ethnic** restaurants give people a chance to taste dishes from around the world. Look in your local phone book. You will find restaurants offering foods that originally came from far away.

Check out the food pyramid at www.mypyramid.gov for more information on food groups and healthy portion sizes.

They may be from Germany, Spain, or Thailand. It is fun and tasty to try new foods, but keep looking for clues. Study the menus carefully to search for healthy meal choices.

Let's say you and your family are trying out a new French restaurant. The food is excellent, but do you really want to eat everything on your plate? Be aware that an average 9- to 13-year-old needs 5 to 6 ounces (142 to 170 grams) of grain, 2 to 2.5 cups of vegetables, 1.5 cups of fruit, 3 cups (710 milliliters) of milk, 5 ounces (142 g) of meat, and 5 teaspoons (25 ml) of fat each day. These should be spread throughout the day, typically in three meals and one or two snacks.

Keep in mind that restaurants often provide more than these recommended portions. When looking at your plate and trying to determine appropriate serving sizes, it often helps to think of common objects you can easily visualize in your head. For example, 1 cup of potatoes, pasta, or rice is about the size of a tennis ball. A 3-ounce (85 g) serving of meat is about the size of a deck of cards. A medium piece of fruit or 1 cup of leafy green vegetables is about the size of a baseball. A 1.5-ounce (42.5 g) serving of cheese is about the size of four stacked dice. And 1 teaspoon (5 ml) of oil is about the size of the tip of your thumb.

As you visit various ethnic restaurants for the first time, healthy eating may seem like a challenge. Many of the foods sound or look unfamiliar, so how can you determine what's best for your body? Keep an eye out for your nutritional clue words! Search the menu for vegetables that are fresh or steamed, and look for meats, poultry, and fish that can be baked or broiled. Request that all dressing and sauces be served on the side. Don't forget to hunt for whole grains either. Depending on the type of ethnic food you're eating, you can find everything from whole grain pasta to whole grain **tortillas**.

Dishes that feature stir fried vegetables are often on the menu at Thai restaurants.

Above all, ask questions. Your server will know what is in each dish and how it is prepared. If you're still not sure how healthy a particular item is or whether or not you'll like it, consider splitting an entrée with someone else at the table.

It's smart to be especially conscious of your calorie intake when you eat out. But how many calories should you consume? Most 10- to 12-year-olds of average size need about 2,000 calories a day, depending on how physically active they are. A very active person burns more calories than someone who is less physically active. If you eat more calories than your body uses in a day, the extra energy will be stored as fat in your body. In other words, you will gain weight.

Your body needs good food to stay healthy. It also needs water—and plenty of it. Did you know that about 60 percent of your body is water? Second only to oxygen, water is necessary for our survival. We can go a month without food but only a week without water.

REAL WORLD MATH CHALLENGE

Taylor's family recently discovered a new Chinese restaurant. The last time they dined there, each person had an order of honey chicken (1,110 calories), hot and sour soup (650 calories), and a soda (200 calories). **Calculate the total number of calories each person consumed.**

Tonight, Taylor's family wants to make healthier dinner choices that have fewer calories and reflect more of the recommended food groups. Each person decides to eat half an order of chicken and mixed vegetables (300 calories), steamed brown rice (120 calories), and 1 percent milk (100 calories). Instead of ordering dessert at the restaurant, they agree to go home and eat 1/2 cup of fresh raspberries (35 calories).

How many calories does each person consume during this meal?

How much of a difference is there in calorie intake between the two meals?

(Turn to page 29 for the answers)

CHAPTER FIVE

BON APPÉTIT!

Many sandwich shops let you choose your ingredients and create your own sandwich.

It may not occur to you as you scarf down a deli sandwich or try salmon **sushi**, but you use math to make healthy food choices. Math and your knowledge of the food groups help you determine what items

"Eat breakfast like a king, lunch like a prince, and dinner like a peasant." This old saying means you should consume the largest number of calories early in the day when you need the most energy. Eat fewer calories as the day wears on. Do you think this is a good idea? Why or why not?

you need to include in each meal. You use math to evaluate appropriate portion sizes, read menus, count calories, and calculate prices.

You're not limited to using your math skills when eating out either. Sometimes it is quicker and healthier to cook your favorite restaurant dishes at home. Some restaurants even offer their products at the market, online, or in the restaurant itself. If this is not the case, get creative!

Do you like tacos? Try preparing a pan of taco filling using lean ground beef or ground turkey, store-bought taco sauce, and fresh onions and peppers. Consider purchasing whole grain taco shells from the store. After you've added the filling, top the finished product with shredded lettuce, diced tomatoes, and low-fat cheese. If you want a side dish, cook up some low-fat canned refried beans or rice flavored with salsa. With a little extra work, you have a nutritious "fast-food" dinner and don't have to wait in line at the drive-through!

If you enjoy restaurant tacos, you might want to try making your own healthy version at home.

If you simply can't stay away from your favorite restaurant, determine whether it has takeout and then order two or three dinner selections. Divide them among four people at home, and simply add whole grain bread or chips, vegetables, and a low-fat dessert. One idea is to pick up an extra-long submarine sandwich from your local deli. Just split the sub four ways at your house, and serve it with a homemade fruit salad and some cold milk.

There are countless ways to enjoy food from restaurants and still make healthy decisions about what you're eating. Math and an understanding of nutrition are both important. These tools will help you care for your body and enjoy your meal as you revisit old restaurants, try new ones, or even re-create take-out food at home. Where will you be dining tonight?

Real World Math Challenge Answers

Chapter One

Page 6

Based on Dr. Doherty's study, 77 percent of meals are not eaten in restaurants.

100% – 23% = 77%

The percentage of meals made at home that did not use convenience foods or takeout items was 57 percent.

26% + 17 % = 43% = percentage of meals that used convenience foods or takeout items

100% – 43% = 57% = the remaining percentage that did not use convenience foods or takeout items

Page 7

Most people eat 21meals each week.

3 meals x 7 days = 21 meals each week

If people eat 23 percent of their meals in restaurants, they eat about 5 meals in restaurants each week.

21 meals x 0.23 = 4.83 meals, or about 5 meals

People eat about 260 meals in restaurants each year.

52 weeks x 5 meals per week = 260 meals

Chapter Two

Page 14

The fettucine Alfredo meal contains 57 percent of Jay's daily calories.

1,140 calories ÷ 2,000 calories = 0.57 = 57%

If Jay had split his entrée with his sister and ordered a mixed greens salad with low-fat dressing he would have consumed 640 calories.

1,140 calories ÷ 2 = 570 calories for half a serving of fettuccine Alfredo

50 calories + 20 calories = 70 calories for the salad and low-fat dressing

570 calories + 70 calories = 640 calories

The meal of ½ the fettuccini Alfredo and the salad with low-fat dressing has 500 calories less than a full serving of fettuccine Alfredo

1,140 calories – 640 calories = 500 calories

Chapter Three

Page 17

The difference in calories between the fries and the apple slices with low-fat caramel dip is 150 calories.

250 calories – 100 calories = 150 calories

The fries contain 12.5 percent of Lin's daily calories.

250 calories ÷ 2,000 calories = 0.125 = 12.5%

The apples and caramel dip contain 5 percent of Lin's daily calories.

100 calories ÷ 2,000 calories = 0.05 = 5%

Page 18

Marcus consumes 3,030 calories by making these meal selections.

500 + 140 + 180 + 420 + 380 + 210 + 380 + 250 + 240 + 330 = 3,030 calories

Marcus consumes 730 calories more on the day he eats all of his meals at the fast-food burger restaurant.

3,030 calories – 2,300 calories = 730 calories

Chapter Four

Page 24

Each member of Taylor's family consumed 1,960 calories the last time they dined at the new Chinese restaurant.

1,110 calories + 650 calories + 200 calories = 1,960 calories

Each member of Taylor's family will consume 555 calories if they make the healthier dinner choices.

300 calories + 120 calories + 100 calories + 35 calories = 555 calories

Each member of Taylor's family will consume 1,405 fewer calories if they make the healthier choices this time.

1,960 calories – 555 calories = 1,403 calories

Glossary

calories (KAL-uh-reez) the measurement of the amount of energy available to your body in the food you eat

consume (kuhn-SOOM) to take in

convenience foods (kun-VEEN-yuns FOODZ) partially prepared food items that decrease the labor needed prior to serving

ethnic (ETH-nik) food prepared according to the customs and traditions of someone's national or cultural background

fettuccine Alfredo (feh-tuh-CHEE-nee al-FRAY-doh) a pasta dish prepared with butter, cheese, and cream

nutritious (nu-TRISH-uss) adding value to one's diet by contributing to health or growth

portion (POR-shuhn) a part or share of something; enough of one kind of food to serve someone at a meal

poultry (POHL-tree) birds that are raised for their meat and eggs; chickens, turkeys, ducks, and geese are poultry

salsa (SOL-suh) a sauce made from tomatoes, spices, onions, and peppers

sushi (SOO-shee) cold rice prepared with vinegar and rolled into rounds with bits of raw seafood or vegetables

tortillas (tor-TEE-uhz) round, flat bread that is made from cornmeal or wheat flour

For More Information

Books

Dalgleish, Sharon. *Fast Food.* North Mankato, MN: Smart Apple Media, 2007.

Turck, Mary. *Healthy Snack and Fast-Food Choices.* Mankato, MN: LifeMatters, 2001.

Web Sites

Check out the Web sites of your favorite restaurants. Many major restaurants list the nutritional value of various menu items online.

American Diabetes Association—Your Guide to Eating Out
www.diabetes.org/nutrition-and-recipes/nutrition/eatingoutguide.jsp
Helpful tips on how to choose healthy meals at restaurants

U.S. Department of Agriculture—MyPyramid.gov
www.mypyramid.gov/
For detailed information on the various food groups and healthy eating

Index

About the Author

Cecilia Minden, PhD, is a literacy consultant and the author of many books for children. She is the former director of the Language and Literacy Program at Harvard Graduate School of Education in Cambridge, Massachusetts. She would like to thank fifth-grade math teacher Beth Rottinghaus for her help with the Real World Math Challenges. Cecilia lives with her family in North Carolina.